What's the Difference Between a FROG and a TOAD?

by Mary Firestone
illustrated by Bandelin-Dacey

Picture Window Books
Minneapolis, Minnesota

Thanks to our advisers for their expertise, research, and advice:

Michelle D. Boone, Ph.D.
Department of Zoology
Miami University, Oxford, Ohio

Terry Flaherty, Ph.D., Professor of English
Minnesota State University, Mankato

Editor: Shelly Lyons
Designer: Abbey Fitzgerald
Page Production: Melissa Kes
Art Director: Nathan Gassman
Editorial Director: Nick Healy
Creative Director: Joe Ewest
The illustrations in this book were created with watercolor.

Photo Credits: Shutterstock/siloto (handmade paper), 1 and
22 (background) and throughout in sidebars and titlebars.

Picture Window Books
A Capstone Imprint
151 Good Counsel Drive
P.O. Box 669
Mankato, MN 56002-0669
877-845-8392
www.capstonepub.com.com

Printed in the United States of America in North Mankato, Minnesota.
032010
005738R

All books published by Picture Window Books
are manufactured with paper containing at least
10 percent post-consumer waste.

Library of Congress Cataloging-in-Publication Data
Firestone, Mary.
What's the difference between a frog and a toad? / by Mary Firestone ;
illustrated by Bandelin-Dacey.
p. cm. — (What's the difference?)
Includes index.
ISBN 978-1-4048-5544-1 (library binding)
1. Frogs—Juvenile literature. 2. Toads—Juvenile literature. I. Bandelin, Debra,
ill. II. Dacey, Bob, ill. III. Title.
QL668.E2F45 2010
597.8'9—dc22
2009006885

What's that leaping near the pond?
It's small and green. It caught a fly!
Could it be a frog? Or is it a toad?

Frogs and toads look a lot alike.
Do you know the differences between
a frog and a toad?

3

Frogs and toads are found in almost every kind of environment, except very cold areas. They live almost everywhere around the world, except Antarctica, the Arctic, and Greenland.

frog

There are about 5,500 species, or kinds, of frogs and toads. But one in three of these animals is at risk of extinction. Humans are to blame. They change or destroy the environment in which these animals live.

Frogs and toads live near ponds, swamps, and marshes. Frogs live on the ground or in trees. Toads live only on the ground.

toad

Frogs and toads belong to the same animal class. They are amphibians. Amphibians are cold-blooded. Their body temperature changes with their surroundings. They are also vertebrates. They have a backbone.

frog

Both frogs and toads have stubby front legs. They are also roughly the same size. In fact, toads are a type of frog.

parotoid gland

toad

Toads have parotoid glands behind their eyes. These glands make poisons that help scare off predators. Some frogs have these glands, too.

Although frogs and toads are usually close to the same size, frogs have slimmer bodies and longer hind legs. Thin bodies and long legs are good for leaping and swimming. Some tree frogs can leap from one tree to another tree.

African frogs are known as great jumpers. Some of them can jump as far as 14 feet (4.3 meters) in a single hop!

Toads are chubbier than frogs. They also have shorter hind legs. Their plump bodies and short hind legs are good for hopping along the ground.

Many frogs have webbed hind feet. Some also have webbed front feet. Webbing makes it easy for frogs to swim. Some frogs, such as tree frogs, have pads on their toes. The pads help the frogs climb up trees or buildings without slipping. Frogs with toe pads can even walk up a glass window.

Most toads do not have webbed feet or sticky toe pads. They walk and hop on land, and rarely swim or climb trees.

Have you ever touched a frog's skin? Most frogs have skin that feels smooth and slick.

A toad's skin is drier and bumpier than a frog's skin.
The bumps look like warts. A toad's skin feels rough.

Some people think you can get warts from touching a toad's skin. But this isn't true.

Some frogs have brightly colored skin. They are usually poisonous. Their bright colors warn predators to stay away.

frog

The golden poison dart frog of Central America is tiny, about 1 inch (2.5 centimeters) long. This frog may be small, but the poison on its skin is very strong.

Many kinds of frogs and toads blend in with their surroundings. When animals match their surroundings, predators have a difficult time finding them. These frogs and toads often have green or brown spotty skin.

toad

Have you ever seen a frog use its tongue to snatch a moth, fly, or grasshopper from the air? Frogs and toads have sticky tongues. The sticky tongues are useful for catching flying insects. Some frogs and toads even eat small rodents, such as mice. Frogs also eat worms.

frog

16

toad

Frogs and toads have tongues that are one-third the length of their bodies. If your tongue was that long, you could touch your belly button with it!

Frogs in cold areas spend winter underground or under leaves with other frogs. Some frogs spend the winter at the bottom of small streams. There the water doesn't freeze because it is always moving.

Toads dig themselves into the dirt or mud until they are completely covered. The mud keeps them warm during the cold winter months.

Spring and summer are mating seasons for frogs and toads. During mating season, the pond is noisy.

After mating season, the pond looks calm. But a lot is going on. Frogs and toads have laid eggs in the water. Many frogs lay eggs in big clusters. Toads lay eggs in long strings.

frog

toad

Eggs laid by frogs and toads will become tadpoles in about six to 21 days. After about three to four months, the tadpoles will become new frogs and toads.

FROG

slim body

smooth, slick
skin

long hind legs

TOAD

parotoid glands

plump body

bumpy, dry
skin

short hind legs

22

Fun Facts

Red-eyed tree frogs lay their eggs on the underside of leaves that hang over ponds and marshes. When the young frogs hatch, they fall into the water below, where they find food and become tadpoles.

The Goliath frog of Africa is the world's largest frog. It can have a body as long as 1 foot (.31 meters).

The American toad protects itself from snakes by puffing up. This way, the frog looks too big to swallow.

When frogs and toads sing all at once, it's called a chorus.

A North American wood frog's body freezes during winter. Its heart slows down, and even stops. In spring, its body thaws, and the frog is ready to swim!

Glossary

amphibian—an animal that can live on land and in water

cold-blooded—having a body temperature that changes with the surroundings

extinction—the state or process of a species dying out

mating—joining together to produce young

parotoid glands—the glands that produce poison in toads and some frogs

pollution—dirty, smelly waste that makes air and water dangerous to living things

predator—an animal that hunts and eats other animals for food

rodent—small mammals with big teeth for chewing; mice, rats, and squirrels are rodents

species—a specific kind of animal with certain characteristics

tadpole—a young frog that swims in water and looks like a fish

webbed—having skin that stretches between the toes

To Learn More

More Books to Read

Bredeson, Carmen. *Fun Facts About Frogs!* Berkeley Heights, N.J.: Enslow Publishers, 2006.

Nelson, Robin. *Pet Frog.* Minneapolis: Lerner Publications Co., 2003.

Parker, Steve. *Eyewitness Pond & River.* New York: DK Pub., 2005.

Slade, Suzanne. *From Tadpole to Frog.* Minneapolis: Picture Window Books, 2009.

Internet Sites

FactHound offers a safe, fun way to find Internet sites related to this book. All of the sites on FactHound have been researched by our staff.

Here's all you do:

Visit *www.facthound.com*

FactHound will fetch the best sites for you!

Index

bodies, 8, 9, 22, 23
cold-blooded, 6
eggs, 20, 21, 23
eyes, 7
homes, 4, 5, 18
legs, 7, 8, 9, 22
parotoid glands, 7, 22
skin, 12, 13, 14, 15, 22
tadpoles, 21, 23

toe pads, 10, 11
tongue, 16, 17
vertebrates, 6
webbed feet, 10, 11

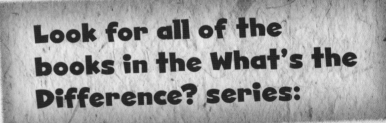

Look for all of the books in the What's the Difference? series:

What's the Difference Between a Butterfly and a Moth?

What's the Difference Between a Frog and a Toad?

What's the Difference Between a Leopard and a Cheetah?

What's the Difference Between an Alligator and a Crocodile?